A Book of Nighttime Poems

STILL·AS·A·STAR

selected by Lee Bennett Hopkins

illustrated by Karen Milone-Dugan

Little, Brown and Company

Boston Toronto London

For Sister Rosemary Winkeljohann—
STAR MAKER
STAR SHINER
STAR KEEPER
— L.B.H.

Sweet Dreams to
Hannah M. and Martha K.
— K.M.

Acknowledgments

Thanks are due to the following for works reprinted herein:

Beatrice Schenk de Regniers for ''Keep a Poem in Your Pocket'' from *Something Special.* Copyright © 1968, 1986 by Beatrice Schenk de Regniers. By permission of the author.

Estate of Norma Farber for ''I Swim an Ocean in My Sleep'' and ''Song of the Moon'' by Norma Farber.

Copyright acknowledgments are continued on page 32.

Compilation copyright © 1989
by Lee Bennett Hopkins
Illustrations copyright © 1989 by Karen Milone

First edition

Library of Congress Cataloging-in-Publication Data

Still as a star : a book of nighttime poems /
selected by Lee Bennett Hopkins ; illustrated by Karen Milone.
p. cm.
Summary: Fourteen nighttime poems by Nikki Giovanni,
Norma Farber, Eleanor Farjeon, Beatrice Schenk de Regniers,
and other well-known poets.
ISBN 0-316-37272-2 (lib. bdg.)
1. Night—Juvenile poetry. 2. Sleep—Juvenile poetry.
3. Children's poetry, American. [1. Night—Poetry.
2. Sleep—Poetry. 3. American poetry—Collections.]
I. Hopkins, Lee Bennett. II. Milone-Dugan, Karen, ill.
PS595.N54S75 1988
811'.008'09282—dc19

87-26859
CIP
AC

10 9 8 7 6 5 4 3 2 1

WOR
Published simultaneously in Canada by
Little, Brown & Company (Canada) Limited

Printed in the United States of America

Contents

SONG OF THE MOON

Song of the moon
going up the sky
is soft as a feather
of lullaby.

Wings are brooding
still as a star
crooning to earth
from high and far.

Birdlings rest
in their oval shell
quiet as bronze
of a silent bell.

Slumber, my dove.
The night is deep,
the dark's a dream
and sound asleep.

Norma Farber

5

NIGHT

Night is a blanket
that covers the small
squirrels and chipmunks
and covers the tall
horses out sleeping
under the tree.
I like the night.
It's a blanket for me.

Sandra Liatsos

7

THE STARS

Across the dark and quiet sky
When sunbeams have to go to bed
The stars peep out and sparkle up
    Occasionally they fall

They dance the ballet of the night
They pirouette and boogie down
In blue and red and blue-white dress
    They hustle through the night

The fairies play among the stars
They ride on carpets of gold dust
And Dawn's gray fingers shake them off
    Occasionally they fall

Nikki Giovanni

MAKE BELIEVE

I made believe fly
A bird so blue
It glowed like sky —
    And up it flew!

I made believe grow
A tree in a wood
With petals of snow —
    And there it stood!

I'd love to pretend
A dragon for fun,
Or an ogre — but if
    I saw one I'd run!

So I'll make up a very
Small elf instead
To sing in the moonlight
    Beside my bed.

Harry Behn

10

MOONSTRUCK

I'd like to see rabbits
under the moon,
dancing in winter,
dancing in June,
dancing around
while twilight lingers
and blinky-eyed stars
look down through their fingers.

I'd like to see rabbits
under the moon,
but I always,
always
have to go to bed too soon.

Aileen Fisher

NIGHT MUSIC

In the night
I heard a loon
laughing low and long
as though he knew
his silver laugh
was an evening song.

In the night
I heard a coyote
crooning at the moon
as though he knew
his wildest voice
sang a night-time tune.

In my bed
I heard myself
sing in starry light
with the loon
and coyote,
a song about the night.

Sandra Liatsos

MAGIC STORY FOR FALLING ASLEEP

When the last giant came out of his cave
and his bones turned into the mountain
and his clothes turned into the flowers,

nothing was left but his tooth
which my dad took home in his truck
which my granddad carved into a bed

which my mom tucks me into at night
when I dream of the last giant
when I fall asleep on the mountain.

Nancy Willard

SKYSCRAPERS

Do skyscrapers ever grow tired
Of holding themselves up high?
Do they ever shiver on frosty nights
With their tops against the sky?
Do they feel lonely sometimes
Because they have grown so tall?
Do they ever wish they could lie right down
And never get up at all?

Rachel Field

18

NIGHT SOUNDS

In the street
        sounds of wheels humming,
        sounds of heels drumming.
Humming and drumming,
Keeping me from sleeping.
In the house
        sounds of words mumbling,
        overhead grumbling.
Mumbling and grumbling,
Keeping me unsleeping.
Far away
        sounds of waves lashing,
        quietly crashing.
Lashing and crashing,
Sweeping me to sleep.

Felice Holman

I SWIM AN OCEAN IN MY SLEEP

Night is dark,
night is deep.
I swim an ocean in my sleep.

Night is filmy,
night is far.
I dream upon an ocean star.

Star five-fingered,
starry fish
let me dream my favorite wish.

Foam be pillow
for my head.
Ocean billow be my bed.

Dream is dark,
dream is deep.
I swim an ocean in my sleep.

Dreaming deep,
sleeping tight,
I swim my slumber sea of night.

Norma Farber

STARS

The stars are too many to count.
The stars make sixes and sevens.
The stars tell nothing — and everything.
The stars look scattered.
Stars are so far away they never speak
    when spoken to.

Carl Sandburg

24

LULLABY

Near and far, near and far,
Over the hill there hangs a star.
Over the star is a slice of moon,
And a cloud will cover them very soon.
Far and near, far and near,
My teddy and I are dreaming here
And over us both my mother is bending,
Crooning a tune without any ending,
Near and far, near and far,
Over the hill there hangs a star.

Margaret Hillert

27

GOING INTO DREAM

Where are you going, child, so far away?
Where you cannot follow to watch me at my play,
Light as a fallen feather floating on the stream
I'm going, going, back into the dream.

What will you find there, child, what will you do?
Something that I cannot ever tell to you.
Quiet as a moth flies across the candle-beam
I'm going, going back into the dream.

Eleanor Farjeon

KEEP A POEM IN YOUR POCKET

Keep a poem in your pocket
and a picture in your head
and you'll never feel lonely
at night when you're in bed.

The little poem will sing to you
the little picture bring to you
a dozen dreams to dance to you
at night when you're in bed.

So —
Keep a picture in your pocket
and a poem in your head
and you'll never feel lonely
at night when you're in bed.

Beatrice Schenk de Regniers

31